The Familiar Stranger

The Familiar Stranger

Lewis Turco

OTHER BOOKS BY LEWIS TURCO

Fiction and Poetry

Wesli Court's Epitaphs for the Poets, 2012
The Gathering of the Elders and Other Poems, 2010
The Museum of Ordinary People and Other Stories, 2008
Fearful Pleasures: The Complete Poems, 2007
The Collected Lyrics of Lewis Turco / Wesli Court, 2004
A Book of Fears, Poems, with Italian Translations by Joseph Alessia, 1998
Emily Dickinson, Woman of Letters, 1993
The Shifting Web: New and Selected Poems, 1989
The Compleat Melancholick, 1985
American Still Lifes, 1981
Pocoangelini: A Fantography & Other Poems, 1971
The Inhabitant, 1970
Awaken, Bells Falling: Poems 1959-1967, 1968
First Poems, 1960

Nonfiction

Dialects of the Tribe: Postmodern American Poets and Poetry, 2012
The Book of Forms: A Handbook of Poetics, Fourth Edition, 2012
La Famiglia / The Family, Memoirs, 2010
Satan's Scourge: A Narrative of the Age of Witchcraft in England and New England 1580-1697, 2009
Fantaseers, A Book of Memories, 2005
The Book of Dialogue, 2004
A Sheaf of Leaves, Literary Memoirs, 2004
The Book of Literary Terms, 1999
Il Dialogo, Italian translation by Sylvia Biasi of *Dialogue,*, 1992
Visions and Revisions of American Poetry, 1986
The Book of Forms, A Handbook of Poetics, 1968

The Familiar Stranger
by Lewis Turco

© 2014 by Lewis Turco

Cover design: Lucy Swerdfeger

All rights reserved. No part of this book may be used or
reproduced in any manner whatsoever without
written permission from the publisher,
except in the case of brief quotations
embodied in articles and reviews.

Published by

~Star Cloud Press~

6137 East Mescal Street
Scottsdale, Arizona 85254-5418

ISBN:

978-1932842-78-4 — $ 14.95

www.StarCloudPress.com

Printed in the United States of America

*Published in celebration
of the Poet's eightieth birthday
May 2, 2014*

For Jean, with love

ACKNOWLEDGMENTS

The author owes thanks and acknowledgment to the editors and publishers of these print and on-line venues for first publication of the poems contained in this volume: *The Andover Review* for "Where Is Jonathan?"; *The Aroostook Review* for "The Harbor"; *Arts in Society* for "Priest of Passage"; *The Bellingham Review* for "Snakes"; *The Carleton Miscellany* for "Captain Hood" and "End of Term"; *The Centennial Review* for "The Last Subway"; *The Cimarron Review* for "Nightpiece"; *College English* for "Summer English" (under the title, "Chaucer, Will, Etc."); *Commonweal* for "Bell Weather"; *The Cream City Review* for "The Skater"; *December* for "Image Tinged with No Color"; *DeKalb Literary Arts Journal* for "Aubade Down East"; *Fine Arts* (Cleveland) for "Summer Stock Rehearsal"; *Hiram Poetry Review* for "The Rider"; *Italian Americana* for "The Point"; *Kansas Quarterly* for "Frost and Amaranth"; *The Louisville Review* for "Driving" and "Running"; *The Magazine of Fantasy and Science Fiction* for "A Great Gray Fantasy"; *The Massachusetts Review* for "Night Song"; *The Michigan Quarterly Review* for "The Stranger"; *The Miscellany: A Davidson Review* for "Botany"; *Modern Poetry Studies* for "The Alley" and "A Talisman"; *M.S.S.* for "Terminal"; *NASSPA Journal* for "The Professor at the Corner"; *New CollAge* for "The Silence"; *The New York Quarterly* for "Life and Death of a Rice Gatherer" and "Strange Death"; *The Northwest Review* for "Mon Coeur"; *Oswego* for "Cicadas" and "Wall"; *Per Contra* for "Autogenethliacum" and "Trinity"; *Phantasm* for "Song"; *Poem* for "The Morbid Man Singing"; *Poetry* for "An Arras Tapestry," "The Children of Rome," and "A Song"; *Sam Houston Literary Review* for "Trees"; *The Saturday Review* for "Columbine and Laurel" and "The Student"; The *Sewanee Review* for "The Bruise" and "The Rising"; *The South Dakota Review* for "Seed in the Wind"; *Spring: The Journal of the E. E. Cummings Society* for "Music"; *Star*Line* for "Charon in New England" and "The Stone"; *Trellis Magazine* for "Choriambic Anacreontics," "Columbian Ode," "A Row of Hedges Revisited," and "Sapphics for April," *Tri-Quarterly* for "The Morbid Man"; *The University of Windsor Review* (Canada) for "Coffee, Black"; *Voices in Italian Americana* for "Breitbeck Park"; *Wind* for "Return Requested," and *Wolf Moon Press Journal* for Winding" which was published under a pseudonym.

"Aubade Down East" was reprinted in *A Sense of Place: Collected Maine Poems*, edited by Lillian Kennedy, Alice N. Persons and Nancy Henry, Westbrook: Bay River Press, 2002;

"Bell Weather" was reprinted in *Anthology of Magazine Verse and Yearbook of American Poetry*, edited by Alan F. Pater, Beverly Hills: Monitor Book Co., 1980;

"Fungology" is from *Poem the Nukes*, edited by Barry Zuckor, Cleveland Heights OH: Hot Doggerel Press, 1983.

"Oswego" was published as a limited edition broadside printed for the inauguration of the Hon. John T. Sullivan as Mayor of Oswego, New York, Oswego: Mathom Publishing Company, 1988.

"Words for White Weather" is from *Poetry: Cleveland*, ed. Alberta Turner, Cleveland: Cleveland State University Poetry Center, 1971.

CONTENTS

I. Home Tunes

Oswego	1
A Great Gray Fantasy	2
The Harbor	5
Wall	6
Breitbeck Park	7
The Skater	9
The Professor at the Corner	11
The Student	12
End of Term	13
Summer English	15
Captain Hood	16
Summer Stock Rehearsal	18
Where Is Jonathan?	20
Return Requested	21
Mon Coeur	22
The Morbid Man	23
Autogenethliacum	25
The Morbid Man Singing	26

II. Talismans

Aubade Down East	29
Sapphics for April	30
Words for White Weather	32
A Talisman	33
The Stone	34
Cicadas	35
Trees	36
Columbian Ode	38
Fungology	40
Botany	41
Song	42
Choriambic Anacreontics	43
Aubade to Say the Least	44
A Row of Hedges Revisited	45
The Rider	46

III. Urban Myths

Nightpiece	49
Terminal	50
Night Song	52
The Alley	54
Coffee, Black	55
Snakes	56
The Last Subway	57
Running	58
The Silence	60
Driving	62
Charon in New England	64

IV. The Stranger's Songs

An Arras Tapestry	69
The Stranger	70
Bell Weather	71
Image Tinged with No Color	72
Seed in the Wind	73
Columbine and Laurel	74
Frost and Amaranth	75
A Song	76
The Children of Rome	77
The Rising	78
Life and Death of a Ricegatherer	79
Strange Death	80
The Bruise	81
Priest of Passage	82
Music	84
The Point	85
The Guest	86
Trinity	88

About the Poet	91

I. Home Tunes

OSWEGO

                    It lies in the curves of the lakeshore.
Across Ontario the last of the sun breathes light
     out of the horizon, turning the clouds shades
          of red to the west. The water darkens,
        splits over the stones where the spiders live,
   where the gulls alight to conceive of evening.

               Hardwoods rise on country roads, their limbs
casting tall shadows into the silence deepening
   among the tumescent milkweed and the cattails.
         A twist of goldenrod runs into fields,
       to the apple orchard fence where ravens
     give voice to the dark quality of waiting.

              The cries of geese are incipient
out of the north, over the great water, the turning
    of another season. The thrust of wings, the high
        call of flight before the changing wind, will
      fall soon to Oswego's waters, send frog
     and salmon deep, beyond ranges of color

that fades now as the light falls onto Ontario,
           and a dream of summer settles along
       the stone coast road like a fleet of waterbirds.

A GREAT GRAY FANTASY

No need to wound
the pride of witches
with dental pumpkins and
cardboard toots one autumnal
eve each year. Why raise the
wrath
of wraiths; why rile
the local spook
or banshee? Let them lie there
sucking the blood of dreams.
You stay indoors.

If
your id needs its lid lifted, flick
a knob in your parlor. You'll
hear electronic chains scrape
and rattle, see
shadows larrup
the Laramie trail and Mike

Hammer's image pound dickens
out of rubber jaws. The
Great Gray Phantom rides
again. Or, one
should say, still: Halloween has
been perpetual now
for several years.

One has been here
in an easy chair
a month oneself, bewitched
(i.e., made stone) by the runes
incanted by fakirs
of Commerce,
greatest of nether lords.
Come, we're bloodless and it's —
what!
Halloween? October
already?
Out, then,
out of coffins;
out on the porch for air,
zombies! The moon's full. Sniff.
What's that wail, werewolves?
No, that window,
and that one, look there,
everywhere one notes tubes
flickering, faces pasted
to squares of grey
glass and gas. The sound!
it's weird: hooves (cloven?), shots,
songs, shrieks (this Is *Your* Life) — what
a devilish din.

What
are those black masses
against the moon?
Whither bound? Gad, brooms! Goblins,
ghosts, wizards, ogres! What's
that banner say? "MARS
OR BUST!" In we

go for a good view.
a mobile camera
rocket's up ahead of them.

THE HARBOR

    They call it a lighthouse,
   but it's really a soundhouse,
  the voice of its foghorn warning boats
of the breakwater shielding Oswego Harbor
    and the mouth of the river.

    The sky above it is a blue
   crystal containing the sun,
  a feathering of clouds and a flight
of gulls assembling and breaking up, landing on
    the breakwater, and shrieking.

    Gulls at the marina
   rock in the wake of a boat
  going too fast. That's what the summer's
done as well. Winter is waiting to fall out of
    blue crystal over the lake.

WALL

    Mist builds a gray wall
Where the lake begins among
      The stones of the shore.

BREITBECK PARK

Another winter has gone up the flue,
        a season painted blue and
            edged in white, the lake
        licking about the edges
of Breitbeck Park two blocks away,

at the bottom of the hill. Jean and I
        have watched our son take himself
            well in hand around
        the bend where manhood listens
to an altogether different

set of tunes and lyrics, if that's what this
        new noise is all about. What's
            there to say? The sun
        dips into Ontario,
sizzling itself to death every

evening, only to rise and walk again
        like Lazarus on Cloud Nine,
            the idea of life
        dawning slowly upon him.
We head for another season:

this one is done for now. Another comes
        loafing along the river,
            asking the fishers
        on the esplanade if they've
had a bite lately, giving them

an early fly or two, a breeze, a gull.
> The buds are waiting to burst
> > upon the scene. Girls
> > sidle their ways through downtown
> striplings, our son among them, cool

as the first frost of autumn waiting there
under the maple trees in Breitbeck Park.

THE SKATER
For Richard Emil Braun

All the surfaces are cold and clear —
    the edge of the sun on snow,
the pond; the blue of the horizon;
    the ice; the sound of the skates.

You have the sense that you can see to
    the bottom. Your movement is
effortless, without impediment
    either to progress or to

vision. Then — you are not sure just when
    or how — there is a thickening
of texture or of color within
    the water, the suggestion

of a shadow. But you are moving
    too fast to make it out — the
coiling, the skirl of mud far below
    your blades. You blink and circle.

Then, when you have convinced yourself that
    the day has not grown darker,
suddenly you are sure: in the water
    there is the form of a monster —

or perhaps a mermaid — swimming. Blink
    again, and it disappears.
But the day has been altered. The pond
    is no longer merely frozen

water. It is a sinister lens
    that focuses deeply. Now
menaces lurk on peripheries.
      Nothing shows itself clearly.

THE PROFESSOR AT THE CORNER

        And so he walks. The leaves lie dimly
            on his mind: let the chill winter
    wind up everything — the campus, the town —
in a big white ball rolling down a hill of years.
                Blame Santa Claus and a green pine
              rooted in the carpet

        for all the opened presents. The young
            have the pretty wrappings: across
the brown lawns they loiter, minds filled with books
and love — bright ornaments of the evergreen. Who
                makes these tinsel bells, these globes of
              allcolor, angelshair,

        textures? — Among the young, the makers
            mingle. They must not be limned in
any kind of twilight, nor are they to
be aureate: there are no wise men in this creche —
            they are the former young who stand
              watching at the corners.

        Therefore they stand or walk, all the turned
            leaves lying darkly on the wind.
    It is cold. The opened gifts contained but
articles: an item for an hour's using,
            or a moment's; a memento.
            The makers mingle with

                the enrapt, the raptured.
The fallen leaves lie coldly on the mind.

THE STUDENT

This student is lost in his books.
I have seen many students lost many ways.
They have been lost in the halls
looking for some door to enter,
afraid to find it because of Minotaur.
They have been lost in words
that fog up their lenses so badly they can't see.
They have been lost in the backstretch.
They have been lost in the woods with some girl
who told her daddy.
They have been lost in my office waiting
for me to come, but I never do.
I have seen many students lost many ways —
even lost in thought, though very few.
This student is lost in his books.
If he looks up, he will find that he is here:
the present is upon him; all books
lead to the present at last, and that is
the key to the maze of words.

END OF TERM

She shoves her head inside my door; she asks
her grade:
           Girl, I no more know your grade than
I know the color of your true love's lust.
It's *I* who tried to tap *your* lock this year.
Like a lover, I stuck out my head to
enter you, to violate that virgin
soil, to plant in that old Garden the fruit
Adam ate and choked upon, but that Eve
relished in her belly.
               No
soap. No potency, rather. Once again
I've spilt my seed upon rocky acres —
my desk blooms instead. Like rectangular
petals, like monstrous lilies blossoming
in topical marshes, these blueboks lie.
Truth was a batch of humble bees this year
butting against hothouse panes. There was no
pollen gotten upon hairy legs.
                     There
is no honey on my lips for you, girl,
not now. Your grade is the grade you wish for:
neither the best nor the worst; not lowly
nor too good to be true; neither evil
nor glorious.

  Your grade is nothing, sweet;
an oval with an opening, empty
within; a receptacle lying on
its side, its contents nonexistent; the
outline of a womb, a cross section of
sterility; the third letter in the
alphabet.
  Cain's initial, not Abel's.

SUMMER ENGLISH

Chaucer has gone on a Guggenheim.
    Down the hall, Dr. Johnson
    thumbs through Boswell to find out about
himself before the summer session.

Most of the doors on this floor are closed.
    Contemporary British and
    American Poetry has
been gone a semester, wandering

through Europe writing himself to keep
    from thinking of the fall's eager
    ears. He knows where most meanings die.
Meanwhile, the grad instructors have gone

to fetch home their degrees: Soph Comp is
    spread all over Cape Cod now, and
    Milton moulders in Paradise
Regained, newly retired, neatly laid

on the shelf by his old wife. She has
    not opened him up in years. No
    one has. I ask you, doors all, shut,
locked, windowless, knobby, fingermarked:

Is this how poets are immortal?
    For answer, a hollow sound plods
    down the hall. Shakespeare looks out a
door, annoyed. He's *sure* he wrote those plays.

CAPTAIN HOOD

>   Driven from Sherwood
> by the Sheriff of Nottingham, bedogged
>   across the moors by gentry
>   and nobility, smoked
>   out of Bristol by the Black Prince,
>
>   Robin wound up on
>   that atoll where Blackbeard found him drying
>   like a cod on a bed of
>   barnacles. For a piece
>   of eight and a noggin of tar rum
>
>   he signed aboard as
>   a common deckhand. But, being that sort
>   of man, he soon found his new
>   Tuck — Bo'sun Reef, his new
>   Little John — Long John now. Not to speak
>
>   of a dandy brig
>   he highjacked on the Main and named, for old
>   times' sake, the Maid Marian.
>   Well, tales are told of good
>   Captain Hood wherever the Jolly
>
>   Roger and tankards
>   are hoisted. Of how he was hounded from
>   the first to the seventh sea,
>   taking from the rich to
>   dispense to the poor till, at last, his

                proud Maid Marian
was found beached and bleaching at the mouth of
              the Father of Waters. Not
        much is left to tell. The
crew had gone, melting into the big

            bayous. But Cajun
songs tell of a gambler in green who rode
            the sidewheelers with a big
                man who carried a pole,
and a renegade priest. They took from

              the Creole dandies
and the planting men, but little gold stuck
            in their gloves — till at last they
                were drowned, some say, though
others spin odd yarns of the plains, three

hooded riders, and a Cheyenne princess.

SUMMER STOCK REHEARSAL

    They move and stand,
      the ingenue and
     the villain. The hero
    has strong arms, blonde hair, brave eyes
with which to spear the bad guy on

        his own moustache. The girl
        looks gratefully into
        love's frank depths and parts her
        lips. Curtain. Exeunt.

They've only begun to rehearse.
  They call this *blocking the script*.
    But what they really
      intend is to give
        it one big push

     so that it will
    fall over on the
   audience — like life. The
playgoers, however, have
a somewhat different viewpoint.

      The fact is, life's too big
      to move with any sort
      of style. It rolls faster
      on its own wheels. Curtain

Rises. Here come Good and Evil.
There goes Innocence downstage
left. Peekaboo, Truth, we
see you. Applause. Sighs.
Home. Tomorrow.

"WHERE IS JONATHAN?"
September 1, 1973

  ...and hanging in the air,
   the spiderplant. The porch,
the people here, the heavy sun
   laid on a mat of haze.
    We talk of lakes — the lake,

   a block away; picnics
    whiling summer down, of
school next week, of what the children
   do, will do, have done. We
   nod the newcomers up

   the stairs, over the toys,
   into the hall yawning
its heat. And in the distances
   sliding and subsiding,
   as pebbles sile under

   and down, five heads bobbing
   in yesterday's lake, then
four bobbing — "Where is Jonathan?"
   He is near the porch, on
   the trike on the lawn, in

   our minds' eyes looming air
   in the heavy sun laid
on a mat of haze whirling down
   the summer among us
   beneath the spider's plant.

RETURN REQUESTED

These things have come in the mail. This floral couch
was wrapped in a telegram that told of an uncle.
This glass-shaded lamp is a favorite of ours:
it fell out of a catalog, but failed to break,
somehow. The rug is soft. It took a large envelope.
This cobbler's bench was stamped with use
when it arrived. We suspect the mailman
used to make shoes. The bed came in a valentine
from one of the humorous aunts, may they rest
in long lines. The telephone arrives each month.
The child, you ask? The child. It was a warm day,
I recall. The mailman was perspiring. His pouch was heavy.
He was invited in to rest. No one saw him leave.
The house came via airmail. It settled
neatly into its patch of lawn. The bank
keeps track of it by means of overflights.
They are punctual. Sometimes a calendar
is dropped, sometimes a butterfly. Each day
is an event. We await our delivery.

MON COEUR

He   will live, hew love. His limb
is   the dove's perch, time's lurching,
a   green waking. No mind's nor world's
fool   — rather, the meadow's madman
who   is spared by wind, whose spirit
has   no ending. He sings everything,
no   one thing. None know his
sense   yet all may understand him.
Of   this bright earth, of bone's and blood's
humor, still he is sky's as well.
That   stone, sterile, in the brown hand of the
poet   shall turn to loam. That stone
is   the world's fruit to be held, hurled in
an   arc, eaten, beaten, driven as an
ass   is driven over the good ground.
Who   is he, this holy man who
thinks with his flesh? He is none but
himself he is no one and he is all,
a   bridegroom, a bride, bird and snake,
priest, prophet, the namer and the sayer.

THE MORBID MAN

                It is the morbid man
who stands and sings
                the grackle in the bone
the worm of fire
                the shire of apples
counties of the blood
                these fiddles in the grass
that bow and strain
                come cloying wasp
which spots the pear
                and buzzing like a clock
settles to suck
                nectar fulsome of
the summer's sun
                the swallow's stitches
in the air a cloth
                of clouds the quilting done
of mist a patch
                of berries for his lips
that split to sing
                the grackle on the limb
the preying gull
                above the tidal river
moving in
                its bed of muck and gravel
up and down
                as eyes move with the willow
in the wind

                the genuflecting alder
mindlessly
                turning its holy leaves
beside the brook
                inquiring of the leeches
on the falls
                what elixirs

what elixirs assuage
                this fever burning greenly
in the fields?

AUTOGENETHLIACUM, 2 MAY 2012

Today I have reached the year my father was
when he died — I was thirty-four, old enough,

one would think, to handle it, old enough
to lose the man I loved more than myself. I was,

I guess, excepting for the dreams. He was
no one I could live up to — I was not big enough

to fill his shoes, nor was I good enough
to outlive the likes of him. I was

not able to believe the things he was
dedicated to: there were not souls enough

for both of us to save. It was enough
for me to save my own, I thought. Or was

it? I could not believe in souls. What was
a soul? The anima in us? I'd had enough

of preachment to last a thousand years. Enough!
My father was belied by the world. I was

unable to understand how good he was
or could be in the face of hell enough

for all the world forever, hell enough
to last any man old as he was.

THE MORBID MAN SINGING

This tone is his,   the stone's song
no other than   brother of his breath,
fang of water,   tongue of the air.
He is life's fool,   and his leaf's fall
looms as the last   laugh at last
at this martyr   and at his art.
But the leaf shall lie   lightly upon him,
its unique symmetry   the summit of song
which he will enter   leaf-fall and winter —
his blood sprung   from rung rock
till the long rain   of time shall spill
over the stars,   stunning their fires.

II. Talismans

AUBADE DOWN EAST

The window opens upon a vocal dawn,
birds pulsing from their coverts — as though they were
    the letters of a startled word — to form
    the fragment of a phrase against the sky.

Morning is parchment touched with a thousand
quills that attempt to utter a tongue so ancient
    of metaphor, so dark, one must gloss it
    newly. Nighthawk gives ground before phoebe;

grass, greening sharply out of falling shadow,
casts jewels before our and the robin's sight.
    The eastern field swells toward the river
    where a smoky crane stalks among darting

things, smooth stones and marsh reed. Shadow's stain
                                   runs like
ink into the alder groves, retreats as one
    of the eagles that nest upon the point
    beats the sea wind moving lightly inland

along the valley. Our eyes are like morning
birds rising out of gullies filled with midnight
    to touch the sun touching the topmost limbs
    of elms and maples as sunlight waxes

and darkness diminishes before vision
and song. Long glancing rays of the eye of dawn
awaken wings, fill all earth's small throats with praise.

SAPPHICS FOR APRIL

"April is the cruelest month," the poet
says. But then what's March, or the other ten, one
wonders? Every month is a moon of mourning,
                              generally speaking.

Born in May, I dread it when April's over.
Here's another birthday I try finessing.
Then comes June beginning the days of summer —
                              maybe it doesn't.

Graduation into the world of working:
fear and trembling for many, but for others
it is time to enter the Golden Years of
                              useless retirement.

Ah! July! The twittering birdies sing you
songs of desuetudinous boredom, or you're
captive in your cubicle while the sun shines
                              elsewhere for others.

August and July — they are sure to taunt you
with vacations over before they've started;
then September tells you to settle into
                              fall for the long haul.

Here's October, skeletons in one's closet
open doors and warn you that here comes weather
stalking through November's perfidious notions.
                              Indian summer

plunges into winter and bleak December.
Holidays depress us and make us wish for
anything besides these unending carols
    dunning our eardrums

in between advertisements. Here comes snowfall —
melancholy buries us in the thermal
January nightmare. And when we look for
    respite from whiteness,

February blows us the kiss of madness:
March debouches into the muddy season.
After this "the cruellest month" continues
    Nature's mandala.

Every month's the cruellest of the dozen,
one way or another. The wheel goes spinning
down the universe till at last we're flung off
    into the silence.

WORDS FOR WHITE WEATHER
For d. a. levy, October 29, 1942 – November 24, 1968

On a gross day, in a green month
once, a child was Summer's lover.
She, heavy with worlds, sent
the child bouquets of amber light. Giver

and taker, she tossed him petals;
in good barter he gave his leman
words shaped like flesh
of fruits: sweet peach, tart lemon,

berryheart whose vine goes
twining with grass. She gave
him this too: a grassblade made
the frost's sickle, lush love

turned root rape, the maggot's
carnal slither. No matter. Her
kiss was decay. Still, his songs
weather the winter.

A TALISMAN
For Dave McLean, too late.

Lead for this talisman. Pure, so that Saturn will live in it. Pure lead.
    Both of its faces are rubbed smooth. On its front, in a star
pentagram, cut with a diamond burin a scythe so that Nabam,
    standing defending his great tau shall be laid under earth,
old as he is — by Oriphiel, angel of Saturday. Our Lord,
    nailed to a T, is the capstone of this coin made of lead,
though he will never appear in his person, but only as backdrop.
    Grave on the opposite face this, in a hexagon star:
REMPHA, surrounding the head of a bull. Without witnesses carve your
    talisman. Wear it in good health. It will keep you from death,
frighten the devil of cancer, leukemia — rot of the white bone.
    Marrow will redden then. Wear this! It will save you and me.
Bear it — your talisman; wear it, my brother. Or carry this poem,
    Dies Saturni, to life's end. It is all I can do.

THE STONE
An Amerindian legend

It will tell you when you have found it —
you will know that this is your stone,
the one that waited for you
on the side of the hill
beneath the oak, the evergreen,
since it was made in the ages before you.

It will say, "You have found it.
I am yours. Pick me up. I am your stone.
For long I have waited for you."
Take it you must, you will.
Beneath its surface you will have seen
already the shape, the shadow of you.

It will tell you to polish it
until the shine sinks deep into the grain,
till it is smooth to the touch
and nothing of the soil
lingers about it — till it is sheen
and gleam. "Now I will show you

where to grind the hole, to place it,"
it will tell you, perhaps in an evening's dream —
the hole round to the touch
through which you will see your soul
beneath the oak, the evergreen —
the very shape, the shadow of you.

When you have labored over it
with wood and flint, stone upon stone,
driven the smooth hole through,
you will wait on the hill
beneath the oak, the evergreen,
until it is time to see you

as others see you. Then you will hold it
in your hand, hefting what is your own,
what was waiting for you
on the earth of the hill
beneath the oak, the evergreen,
until it was time to see you.

Then you will take and hold it
to your eye; you will look through the stone,
and you will see you
as only others may perceive you —
clearly, without sheen
or aureole. And the stone will free you.

CICADAS

The day is so still
their voices drill into stone —
 cicadas calling.

Did it shrill until
it became only echo,
 this cicada shell?

TREES

Yellow bird, the yellow bird's lying
Along the wind, under the green tree.
The cherry is in blossom under the green tree,
And the wind is flying.

Night hawk, the night hawk's calling
Along the wind, over the dark tree.
The apple is bearing in the dark tree,
And the wind is falling.

Black bird, the black bird's a-wing
Along the wind, beside the bright tree.
The acorn is dropping beneath the bright tree,
And the wind is rising.

Red bird, the red bird's burning
Along the wind, from tree to tree.
The snow is whining through the bare tree,
And the wind is turning.

COLUMBIAN ODE

I.

When *Columbia* broke up in the skies over the western states
February the first, 2003, everyone watched the tape
Loop repeatedly. We sat in the web spun by the spider once
More, as often we'd done since the defunct century flushed itself
Down historical tubes: maybe we knew nothing would come to pass
After all in our dim consciousness. What happens when we expect
Something, usually? Not much. It's the bad joke of the Laughing God
Who will wait while the Earth spins in the dark spaces between his toes
Till the moment we least look for any tragedy. Then he hits
Hard. We think that we've grown — harder than nails, shields that
      surround our souls!
What a joke! We are knocked flat on our broad backs and discover once
More how vulnerable Man is to Fate's blows. We are fragile still.

II.

No song is sung or elegy spoken as
Great sorrow settles over a tragedy,
    Falls into chasms opened into
        Misery. How shall we find our mourning's

True voice in keening, hopeless despair, or in
Wounds newly suffered — coins to be squandered on
    Grief governed not by thought but feelings?
        Time is required for grief to ripen

Into melody, into sorrow's music.

III.

Into melody, into sorrow's music
There will quietly steal another lyric
After all of the requiems have ended,
After most of the mourners have departed.
It will be but a bar or two of heartbeat
Just at first, but a murmur in the bloodstream
Building finally to a constant drumming
Running through the aortas to the fingers,
To the toe-tips and belly. It will be like
Springtime touching the edges of a frozen
Mountain rivulet which, in its descending
Over gradients of downland, brings renewal
To the valleys below. The world begins to
Stir again and the eyes begin to open
Onto vapors arising over waters
Lying under the glimmering of daylight.

FUNGOLOGY

If it were
ever difficult
to grow mushrooms,
it is no longer so. All that
is needed is a space of darkness, with minds
of similar quality and caliber. Given these,
fungi will sprout almost anywhere.
They are very simple to nurture.
Instantly there will
be a wilding garden
of
f
u
n
g
i

which one may enjoy, if but briefly.

BOTANY

You know what I know.
I will not tell you about it.
Let it be a surprise.

It is down there.
It is a flower
with flanged petals.

It is eating something,
something with legs.
It makes almost no sound.

If you go into it,
go without struggling
and it will let you see.

There is a white center,
suns and darkness,
and there is no edge.

SONG

There is a song to sing, but I do not know it.
I heard it once in the long grass,
And again where the moon moved,
But it is long since, as the wind is long.

There is wind to feel, and I have felt it
Moving through the long grass
Under a moon that touched and wavered,
But it is long since, and the moon has moved.

There is water to drink in a dark pond.
I touched it once through the long grass,
And in it the moon wavered,
But it is long since, as the wind is long.

There is a woman to love, and I have known her.
I touched her once, in the long grass
Where the moon wavered in the water,
But it is long since, and the moon has moved.

CHORIAMBIC ANACREONTICS

If we love wine, then what shall be
Done with women? with all those who are left high on the pedestal?
May we love them as well? Or must
Sights be lowered to knee height or perhaps less -- to the sisterhood
Of the streets? No! Surrendering
Love for drink's a mistake not to be brooked! Capture the pair of them!
She will love wine as well as a
Man does women and good wine! We may both revel in love and wine
Till the dawn breaks the window and
Daylight drowns all our sweet dreams of debauch, laurels us all with rue.

AUBADE TO SAY THE LEAST

Morning — a dull silver. The fields
    are an ore of straw. The
rust of maples and oaks fires this
gold of August in our falling —
    and the house is adrift,
running through the sluice of dream. Now,
evening is over on its way
toward windows like quicksilver.

A ROW OF HEDGES REVISITED

Looking out of the high school classroom window
I could see a row of declining hedges
That extended past the frame of the window
Into who knew what that lay awaiting us.
That is a decent image! I remember
Thinking, *one I can drape my senior essay
Over with a minimal effort.* So I
Did. I wrote "A Row of Hedges," submitted
It and waited. One can loiter overly
Long. It has been a lifetime. Looking down that
Ancient hedgerow from this new vantage, one can
Almost see the place where it has its ending.
There is mist behind me. Shadowy figures
Flicker in and out of focus. Have I been
Dreaming of metaphors and similes for
Living all of these years? And am I sitting
Still in adolescent bemusement, waiting
For the hedge to wither, for the daydream to
Die in a fall beyond the darkened window?

THE RIDER

He rides a dark stallion.
He holds a vermilion banner.
His hand is a hand of bone, white bone,
Ivory upon the rein,
And he rides alone.

He rides a dim stallion.
At his side is a blade of steel.
His brow is a brow of bone, white bone
Beneath the iron helm,
And he rides alone.

He rides a black stallion.
On his chest is a corselet of rust.
Through the mail one can see the bone, white bone
Clasping a cage of air,
And he rides alone.

Lost is the name of his stallion,
And the name of his blade is *Hours*.
His pace is the gait of bone, white bone.
He hums like the wind as he wanders,
And he rides alone.

III. Urban Myths

NIGHTPIECE

    It is time to be awake. The clock
turns its face into shadow. The pendulum
        swings across its arc behind night's flowers.

    Elsewhere, blood blooms in the jungles. Each chime
falls upon the carpet and disappears like
        rain or tears. I dream of those who would love.

    It is no time for dreaming. Ratchets and
wheels, the hands of silence move behind my eyes.
        I am awake and helpless. The men in

        their houses with their women are sleeping.
Their kitchens drowse while a world is turning its
        face against the sun. How shall I tell them?

    How shall I say so it will be heard, Wake!
It is a new age! Death must have a meaning,
        not a slogan! Listen to the gong that

        strikes numerals into waste! But the lamp
glows on my table, my chairs seat emptiness,
        the streets lead from our doors to other streets

        till we are webbed and hunkered among our things.
Elsewhere, blossoms fall and fade like reports from
        silence. Age turns into ages. Chimes reach,

like lianas, from life to death, room to room.

TERMINAL

                There is a short line
at the ticket window. Two buses
          wait at the curb outside,
     motors running. The drivers,
drinking cokes near the coin machines,

        check out the women.
Beyond the speckled plate glass window
        late afternoon drizzles.
   The sky matches the color
of the drivers' uniforms.
               She

         stands near a wooden
bench. The drivers have looked her over,
       and their eyes have slid past
       to a flirt dressed in a green
   pantsuit.
       "Now, don't forget to feed

         the cats," she tells him.
She licks her lips, pulls her coat closer
      at her waist. The children
    sit on the bench beside him —
the boy is looking at the bus,

        the girl is crying.
He nods, staring at the floor — it is
     muddy.
           "Have a good trip,"
  he says.

          "They're starting to load.
     We better get going, I guess."

                    He nods. He gets up,
      carries the suitcases out, then stands
                    waiting in the exhaust
          and rain until his son waves
     from his seat behind the window.

NIGHT SONG

    The man is sleeping. He has left
    the washroom light on. His suitcase
lies open on a folding aluminum stand. In the closet
    with its door ajar his suit hangs in the dark.

    The bedclothes are coiled and twisted.
    The mirror is cracked. It reflects
the window dimly. The drapes fold themselves and fall past
                                  the chipped sill
    toward the floor, the carpet that looks mostly

    gray. The noises of the city
    sound like night sliding with the air
over the sill, between the folds of cloth, or like the night's
                                            echoes.
    The sleeping man shifts again, as though he is

    dreaming. His eyes crack open, then
    close again. When the cry that woke
him comes once more, he starts and sits up, staring. His
                                  palms are pressed flat
    against the sheet. He listens; it comes again

    from somewhere down the corridor —
    a fist striking bone; a woman's cry.
Then someone knocking on a door, another woman calling, "Oh,
    no, I know what you two are up to. Let me

    in!" The sound of another blow.
    Another cry. Some choked words, but

no man's voice. The man in the bed has not moved, but his
                                            eyes are stuck
  to the telephone on the nightstand. "Let me

    in," and the rapping of knuckles
    on wood. Teary noises, a door
opening and closing. Muffled sounds sifting through the walls.
                                                    The man
    in the bed does not move for a long time. Then
    he lies down, his hands behind his
    head on the pillow. He stares through
the shifting murk at the ceiling a long way over him. The sounds

    of the dark city crawl in through the mirror.

THE ALLEY

        The fog drifts. I have come out
        of my cocoon of lamplight
    into the mist that sifts through the streets.
    In the alley there are cans and rags
    and I consider them, for there is
little more to consider in the fog.

    If one should speak loudly in doorways
    the knobs would not answer and the sounds
    one's lips formed would fade among dusty
ledges of sandstone, windows and bottles.
        Beneath my steps the street moves,
        but I remain still. Are there

    no others behind the doors
    facing on these avenues?
Will no one come and see time's labyrinth
    winding down the corridors of mist?
    I walk and there is no sound, no sound
    as of footsteps or of knobs turning.

COFFEE, BLACK

It is a dark corner of the city.
          There is one arc lamp shining
      across the street from the drugstore
with its neon sign in the window.

There are no cars. The only thing moving
          in the road is a large sheet
      of newsprint — its corner vibrates
in a breeze snaking along the curb.

The yellow light picks out of the sidewalk,
          where it is in shadow, white
      highlights — cigarette butts, candy
wrappers. In the distance there is sound,

a transformer droning an insect song.
          The light filling the drugstore
      spills through the plate glass storefront,
washes over gumblots and oilstains.

Inside, there is a row of vinyl stools,
          a soda fountain counter.
      A man dressed in a soiled jacket
sits stirring a cup of cold coffee.

SNAKES

>   After she has taken the drug
> she begins to feel them slithering
>   on her skin. They are cool and smooth.
>   Their tongues flicker, testing the air.
>   If they were real, she would be
>
>   terrified. She forces herself
> to remember the dose. She brushes
>   them off, and they disappear as
>   they touch the floor. She breathes, relieved,
>   and begins to let herself
>
>   drift with the trip. She closes her
> eyes, and one drops from the ceiling to
>   her face. She nearly screams. It moves
>   over her lips, across her chin,
>   passes a loop around her
>
>   throat. It begins to squeeze. She knows
> it isn't really there. But then
>   she knows the bed's not there either,
>   nor the room, the radio music
>   in the night air, nor the air.

THE LAST SUBWAY
In memory of Tony Walters

                The train is early;
                its single eye stabs down the rails.
There is only one passenger waiting
            on the platform — thin and dark,
      he is young, his body strung like wire.

                The concrete platform
                is splotched with gumblots. The posters
on the tile walls are covered with wise-
            cracks; they are shredding. Nedick's,
      behind him, is empty, brightly

                lighted, the coffee
            simmering on the hotplate. The cash
register reads no sale, and the sharp sound
            of a bell rung seems to hang
      in the night air heaving its way down

                the stairs from the street.
      He enters the empty car, takes
a strap, stands looking out of the window.
                The door closes. At the end
      of the bar something dark stains the floor.

RUNNING

        In the dream I am
      running. I am looking
          for something — my car,
              parked God knows where,
in the City of Recall:

      the cinema gone
    dark with the flickering
        hours, the candy store
           next door, spiders
in the windows. My legs are

      lead, there is no air;
    something I cannot see
        breathes in the alley.
           As I draw close
to what it is I'm seeking,

      the elm of childhood
    spreads its limbs again, grass
        grows between the flags
          over its roots,
the church my father preached in

      peels in the sunlight.
    My car is parked again
        under the shattered pear,
          and if I could,
I would move my feet to run

       heart pumping, slowing
   like an old film flickering
         over a story
              that runs backwards
when I stop and close my eyes

        to catch my breath.

THE SILENCE
*"The joke fell so flat, you could have driven
a truck through the silence." — Milton Berle.*

      You could have driven a truck
through the silence. You might have felt
      the miles peeling off the road
          under the raddled moon —
      you could have cared less,

      maybe, but then again, you
might have stopped at nothing. Instead,
      the neon light might have buzzed
      in the dark sizzling as
          you stepped down from the

      cab. Then you may have gone in,
sat down at the counter.
                 She could
have been bending down over
      the juke box, the record
      blue in the heavy

      air. You may have ordered, say,
coffee. She might have been blonde. You
      could have heard a cup drop. She
          might have sat down, opened
      her purse, taken out

   a cigarette.
      You could have
stirred your bones, offered her a light.
   You may have been tired, too tired
     to notice her nails — red,
      enameled, edgy

   as she sipped her drink and smoked.
You should have gone into her eyes
    and noticed there the quiet
      miles of summer, the dust
       of darkness, the moons
    turning among the clouds like
rags over the road.
      Instead, you
could have pushed your rig out of
    the tar lot, back onto
      the blacktop and aimed

  your gaze along the white lines
uncoiling in your headlamps. You
   could have cut the silence with
    a radio.
    You felt
   like kicking yourself

  to keep awake as you drove
for Cleveland, or Oswego, or
   home — wherever. You might be
    thinking of her...but then
     again, you may not.

DRIVING
"Dying is a wild night and a new road." — *Emily Dickinson.*

    He had never seen this road before,
could barely see it now past the wipers
threshing on the windshield. The radio
was thorny with static — he turned it off,
but most of the noise continued, the sound

    of torrents on the roof, rain and hail.
He lit a cigarette, the red target
of the dashboard lighter warm in his hand.
He thought he had better stop, but his foot
pressed harder on the accelerator:

    A sheet of water splattered over
the hood; the engine coughed, then caught again,
ran smoother than ever. His headlamps lit
the rain like rods of glass. It was evening,
but not yet dark — he caught a highway sign

    with a glance just as he was passing,
nearly jerked the wheel to see more clearly,
but steeled his arm in time. His muscles felt
like cable, his hands like clamps on the wheel.
He leaned forward and tried to see the road,

    the dashes up the center, the green
islands, the overpasses flashing by.
He glimpsed the yellow markers in the nick,
blinking through the twilight. He swerved and stopped,
skidding in the gravel of the shoulder.

The motor died. He sat and trembled.
"Why am I doing this?" he asked himself.
"What road is this?" Where had he started from,
where was he bound? He tried to shake his head,
but the patterns of the shivered windshield

froze his eye until the darkness fell.

CHARON IN NEW ENGLAND
Casco Bay, Me., Jan. 15, 1977 (AP) "—As the Abenaki neared the ferry landing, Capt. Thurlow looked through tiered, bloodshot eyes and said, 'I feel great. I could do this forever.'"

He stood in the wheelhouse, steering
carefully to dodge the hundreds of clumps
    of ice. "Everyone thinks I'll go
      out of my mind — from the boredom,"
        he said, easing the steel wheel

    through his weather-roughened hands. "But
it's impossible to get bored. Weather
    changes the view every minute,
    and I never get tired of it."
        The bow pushed the black water

into the mist.
            There was no sound,
not even the cry of a tern. The folk
    in their gray hoods sat bowed along
    the gunwale.
           He pointed to a seal
    pup on an ice floe and said,

"It's beautiful out here, but
the waters are tricky. You've got to keep
    your eyes open all the time." But
    there was no time. One could not see
      the eyes of the passengers,
        lost as they were in shadow. "It's

simple," he said. "The people can't be left
      stranded." As the *Abenaki*
   neared the ferry landing,
         he looked through tired, bloodshot
      eyes. "I feel great," he said. The wind
was bitter. "I could do this forever."

IV. The Stranger's Songs

AN ARRAS TAPESTRY

     In clockstruck Arras stars
come broaching the frames where grave
folk lie waking. In the least

     of rooms, stretched among sheets
and chimes, body like the weft
of an old design, there lies

     the beginning of the
gravest — a child threading dreams
as shadows loom and shuttle

     in the stone shires.
In the hempen hours, grieving
for light among his graylings,

     flesh taut upon the bed-
frame, boneframe, stead shaking in
shadow, he shall pass beneath

     the steeples' bobbins
tracing dream and age upon
a warp of hours — all folk

     woven in the tapestry
of town and star: for silence
shall comb this waking and his

     sleep, the gathered umber
be raveled, strand and chime.

THE STRANGER

The world sings with foxes, plover
in the fields, leaves falling the long
route down, and in the hills
mist over the lakes where fish
say the fell thing to the man in the mud,
the face of ash drowning forever
and forever rising, his eyes another
color each time, his face the face
of the stranger forever, born always
the same stranger, brother of the fish,
father of mist, the fields his plow's
share, he and the red leaves,
farrow and cover, bide as the foxes
call in the wind.

BELL WEATHER

Trees file along curbs. Shrub-faces,
   lilac ears listen to dusk
      coming over the lawns.

Indoors, dust weaves its motes among
   coleus and pepper plants.
      Spring slides under the door,

and the phone rings once, its bell hung
   in the heart of dim weather.
      Gray walks from its mousehole

across the rug. Soon a river
   of stars will spill overhead,
      breach dawn, noon, dusk and fall

into a field of goldenrod
   near the blue spruce whose needles
      knit and ravel darkness.

IMAGE TINGED WITH NO COLOR

I smell you coming
with the January wind
buried in your bones, old man,
like a blear of snow in the pines.

Is she your sister,
or your mother, whom I see
dressed in an ice blue shawl,
sweeping the leaves before you?

Often I have thought of you
when the sun strikes aside
the dark leaves like so many webs
spun across the day to tangle my eyes,

and always your image
is tinged with no color, no
touch, only a scent
as of asters lying under a fallen clock.

In your pockets, I can tell,
there are small things wound in pelts —
mice, perhaps, or squirrels
nesting against the chill flesh of your thighs.

I smell you coming, by night,
a skein of white planets
unraveling behind you,
and as you pass I shall greet you coldly.

SEED IN THE WIND

In the interstices of final
and prime seasons, the white sun
glints in a puddle, paling like a jellyfish
thinking of nothing.

In the air the God of Cheeks
pauses to swallow a seed,
and in that seed there are
fourteen grackles and a jay

flirting with beginnings.
A feather stuck in the wind starts
to write a sentence,
but the clouds erase it, and

nothing has been said,
though some mad beetle
has a scurrilous tale to tell
earlier on in the old grass.

The watcher in the window stabs
out of his glass like a blade
that cuts nothing; his eyes are eaten
by distance. That sad, vague

animal called by the name of wishes
stirs and startles in his veins,
and if he were snow today he would be snowing,
and his chill heart would put forth leaves.

COLUMBINE AND LAUREL

Damoiselle, those white limbs genuflecting
before you as you push
that instrument through the forest,
bend but to stroke

the keys of your marimba
with the lightest of mallets.
I can hear you coming
like a freshet through stones,

with a step soft as mole's wool.
My ears are like throats
savoring your ivory cantata.
Your feet are words buoyant

in an ocean of moss —
ah! what a phrase they trail
down the mountain.
You are columbine and laurel sprung from snow,

you come singing from the old time,
your song blue, your eyes gray as lichen,
your hands ten stings of gnats
in the chapel of my brow.

FROST AND AMARANTH

And this shall be the flower:
frost and amaranth,
the dwelling apart and the bloom
turning in its sphere.

A SONG

The ravages of the worm are slow
in the mortal shock. The swift pincers
manipulate small feasts
behind our sick eyes: the animal
exudes shadow. It is the sunrise

which baffles. Recall a child at dawn
sinking in the grass into the sea
of morning, light spun out of dew about him
in tides and spangles. Where is he now,
that sailor of light? Look inward — he

is drowning in blood, a minuscule
leviathan wound round him feeding
on time seeping from his veins. Should you ask why
a man sings this foul song in your ear,
it is no man, but the child screaming.

THE CHILDREN OF ROME

The children suckle at the wolf.
All paths lead to these seven hills
where the lambs and goats graze among old
stone. The saints, the orators
have quarried flesh here from the centuries.

The flocks have been known to rise,
their soft lips furling from the white edge
of their hunger, crazed by the wine
let from their veins, to butcher
the butcher in his charnel house.

The ages age in this abbatoir
of catacombs and naves. Hours,
sins, toils of the ambitious: flags,
fish, and crucifixions. You shepherds!

Consider these roads, these ewes and rams,
the lambs shorn to clothe holy Tiber
in ragwear, Romulus tearing
at the wolf's dugs, ayes afire — consider
Remus, his hands crooked in the foul hair
of the Mother of us all.

THE RISING

Who must it be, this player of nocturnes?
Whom shall he behold,
the keys plunging into dwale
and rising through the spheres to light?
In none so much as a paling and unfolding,
the listener awake out of his sleep,
threads looming in the shuttle,
each several designs of one fabric,
the shoe upon the last,
the end in its birth,
peacock and dove lost till they be owned
in one cerement and swaddling.
Listen, for under the chords there lies silence:
only that which speaks
and nothing more.

LIFE AND DEATH OF A RICEGATHERER
from the Lithuanian of Algimantas Mackus,
with Ceslovas Melsbakas

Though my hands were soiled coal-black
and my eyes — "not the waters of those plantations"
(so I was told as he came riding by,
that young shepherd, so young and handsome) —

still I knew that, as they rode by,
no one ever spoke truly near those waters,
that no one believes the glassy words
of a shepherd on horseback riding by.

So little! Such a few handfuls of rice,
and such a little of life!
In the expanses of that plantation, as it was raining,

I gathered life in my hands...
and that shepherd rode back
to her — covered with cloth and rice.

STRANGE DEATH
*from the Lithuanian of Algimantas Mackus,
with Ceslovas Melsbakas*

Once only I marveled at the spring
and that night went to earth,
oh the dew was greening
greener than all else in the spring!

I was felled, and none lifted me
nor roused me in the rainfall,
only weeds and blades gathered round,
stood stunned that man

could fall in springtime
in the scented rain descending.

THE BRUISE

Is it not too great a will that birds falter
or that we fail
the mind a circle, the heart a dead calm?
Just so, unjust in these things:
the bruise becoming flesh, all the world
fastening upon us, upon itself,
and within the need walking away
into the leaf, the feather,
waking us away from were
into shall be, the blue lord
who remarks the dove
as it rises into stone, the circle of lignite
and dross. So it shall fall to us,
forever the arc forever fair.

PRIEST OF PASSAGE
(*for William Golding*)

A Mouse:

I lie here in the root of this weed, gray
as the rest of the night. I hear the sharp
points of the stars spearing the undergrowth.
The nails of my hands grasp thistle and moss
as I listen, my cold eyes glistening.

An Owl:

He is down there, waiting. He will not hear
my wings until they are beating his sides,
until my talons have wound his life in
spools of flight and the earth diminishes
as his world grows smaller, washes at last
into the wells of his sight. Let him wait
as I circle in a white storm of stars.

The Mouse:

I think I hear him, but I do not hear
him. I only think. What I do hear is
the hoofsong of the nightwind rearing like
a stallion among the boles and cones. Branches
beat against branches — a flock of beaks sharp
as this blade of sawgrass against my ear.

The Owl:

It will be soon now. All I need do is
circle, draw the spiral sign once more on
the slate of silence. I am priest of his
passage, a monk who dwells in his bowels.
I finish the gesture thus: the tip of
my wing lances the moon with this gesture.

The Mouse:

Stars and a tide of wind.

The Owl.:

                    Up. We are one.

MUSIC

There is music
In the way a leaf turns
Its silver side to the wind,

And there is an image
In silence stealing
Down from the eaves
To cover blades with dew.

If only we could hear
The colors of space
When we look up
Into nothing between the stars,

Being would be a child's smear painting
Falling out of the bell of an oboe.

THE POINT

   What is the point of life,
the wind whining in the pines,
   sighing at times, singing
otherwhiles, the leaves whirling
   in whorls like flying sheaves,
   sorrowing grievously
   for the fall of the year?

   What is the point of this
burrowing and scurrying,
   all of this fluttering,
soaring aloft, scattering,
   sifting through sandgrains,
   mating and bothering
   to breed, begin seeding

   over again over
millions of failings, of falls
   and arisings, springs for
ever, never despairing
   of anything to ask,
   "What is the point of life?"
   Life is the point of life.

THE GUEST

      "Ah! There you are," he said,
turning his head as Death walked through the door,
      "I've been waiting for you.
      What's taken you so long?"

      Death did not reply. "Please,
have a seat. You're looking rather drawn. You
      must be tired. Have you been
      busy lately?" He laughed.

      "What a question! Of course
you have. Have you traveled far?" He cleared his
      throat nervously as Death
      sat down before the fire.

      Embers glowed In the grate.
Outdoors rain fell out of the autumn dusk.
      Death was silent staring
      at the coals. "Can I get

      you anything?" He asked.
Shadow stood in the doorway. Death did not reply.
      Moments lengthened. The clock
      measured them stolidly.

      He took a seat himself
and stared at his guest until at last he
      wavered and cleared his throat
      again. At last he stood.

"Well, is it time to go?
It's gotten rather late I think, don't you?"
    The rain fell quietly,
      embers glowed in the grate,

yet Death did not reply.

TRINITY

I. *The Big Bang*

•

II. *The Big Blink*

  Is it a butterfly or a wasp? No matter,
     catch it in our net – don't let it get away:
When life blinks out, that's it: Nothing existed, ever.
     The Big Blink takes place. There's nothing to regret,

  no one to regret it. There will be no darkness —
     darkness so deep we are of it, no silence
so vast one can hear oneself think, nothing to wish for,
     nothing to want, no one to think or wish for,

  no darkness or silence so vast and deep that we
     are the silence, nor so deep and vast *we* are *of*
it, nor *in* it, nothing to want, no self to wish
     or wish for, no being to become, to Be.

III. *The Big Blank*

About the Poet . . .

by LINDA LOOMIS
reprinted by permission from *Oswego*, an Oswego State alumni publication

Nose stuck in a book, wandering in words while his feet trod the streets of Meriden, Connecticut, Lewis Turco walked deliberately on a path that led to his career as a poet and professor.

"I loved to read when I was a kid," he says. "I felt that I would like to give to others the delight those authors gave to me. I decided to try to become a writer myself."

Having defined his course, in characteristic manner, he set out. At 15, while in prep school, he took third place in a local newspaper's high school short story contest. A job as student correspondent and newspaper morgue clerk ensued at that same paper; he began submitting poems to the local poetry column, and his literary career was launched.

Four years in the U. S. Navy after high school put Turco on the *USS Hornet* for two years and a round-the-world cruise. Before his release from active duty in 1956, he married Jean Houdlette, and made plans to attend the University of Connecticut, with two scholarships from the Meriden newspaper he had worked and written for which augmented his G. I. Bill. With Navy-earned academic credits, and with a list of publications more impressive than that of some of his professors, Turco's UConn program was accelerated and the military money also covered an M.A. from the Writers' Workshop of the University of Iowa.

Teaching at Fenn College after graduation, Turco founded and directed what is now the Cleveland State University Poetry Center, (now more than half a century old), an accomplishment that brought him to the attention of Oswego's Dr. Erwin Palmer, who was chair of the English department.

"Dr. Palmer wanted an actively publishing poet, and he wanted me to start a poetry center modeled after the one in Cleveland," Turco says. "I had to tell him it was impossible in a city the size of Oswego."

Turco offered an alternative. "I said I could begin a program in writing arts if he wanted it." With that, Oswego became the site of one of the premier undergraduate writing programs in the nation. Genre specific and workshop oriented, the program demands academic rigor with commitment to creativity and publication. As director and professor, Turco shaped student authors at Oswego for 31 years before he retired in 1996.

Poets around the world, not just students at Oswego, have been initiated into the principles of formal poetry through Turco's *The Book of Forms*, now in its fourth edition. Wesli Court (change those letters around for an a-ha! moment) published *Epitaphs for the Poets* in 2012, and Turco last summer finished an epic poem titled *The Hero Enkidu*.

A series of byways broadened his original destination to include titles of "founder" and "director" and "publisher," but Turco has never taken a detour. Fifty-two books, chapbooks and monographs, in addition to hundreds of poems, stories, plays and essays in journals and anthologies, are evidence of his status as a writer. Generations of former students attest to his effectiveness as a professor.

www.ingramcontent.com/pod-product-compliance
Lightning Source LLC
LaVergne TN
LVHW041341080426
835512LV00006B/555